The Essential Elizabeth Brewster

Table of Contents

---

*   These poems date from the 1950s but did not appear in book form until 1977.

Foreword

In Elizabeth Brewster's poem 'Cloud Formations', the speaker recalls her eight-year-old self reading 'Shelley's Cloud poem', how for the first time 'I heard a voice / felt the wind blow / riffling my hair, / the poet's ghost breathing / changing my life forever // knew even then / I too must try / must find the words / must play the game / of "pass it on"...' (*Entertaining Angels*, p. 7). Brewster is referring to her own childhood epiphany, the way it compelled the girl saving cut-out poems in a scrapbook to become a poet whose body of work spanned much of the 20th century and well into the next.

But first Brewster had to surpass the uncertainty of her upbringing. Born in a New Brunswick village in 1922, between two World Wars, she suffered frail health, and her family's poverty and frequent moves interrupted her schooling. Still, she was a precocious reader of whatever presented itself, including the copy of Robert Burns's poems her father gave her, her mother's Bible, Shakespeare, *The Scarlet Letter* (by age seven), books she found in the houses her mother sometimes cleaned, even the Eaton's catalogue. She came to view books, pencil and paper as 'dependable friends' (*The Invention of Truth*, p. 10), and soon her aspirations turned toward writing.

Adolescence 'let loose a flood of poems' (p. 6), one of which her father surreptitiously submitted to Saint John's *Telegraph-Journal*, when she was twelve. It marked her first publication, and though she resented his not having asked for her permission, she was pleased to see her words in print. During high school a poetry competition she entered proved to be a pivotal moment — she travelled to Saint John and met one of the judges. P.K. Page was only six years Elizabeth's senior and she encouraged the young writer. Later, with an entrance scholarship in hand, she attended the University of New Brunswick (UNB), engaging with writers A.G. Bailey, Fred Cogswell, Donald Gammon, Robert Gibbs and Desmond Pacey, and played an integral role in the 1945 founding of the long-standing literary journal *The Fiddlehead*. She went on to earn three more degrees, including a Masters from Radcliffe, Harvard's women's college. In the poem 'Harvard-Radcliffe Daze', she writes of attending readings given by Robert Frost and T.S. Eliot (the latter introduced as the 'greatest living poet') and of her renewed ambition: 'I too planned to be a poet — / Maybe even (such is youthful arrogance) / The Greatest Living' (*Wheel of Change*, p. 83). Yet she simultaneously wonders how someone like her could be so presumptuous as to set her own talent 'next to all that tradition'. She felt keenly the obstacles of her gender and poor, provincial background; she was excluded from male-only reading rooms, as well as from scholarships and support systems. Nevertheless, even when her output slowed during the nomadic job-to-job years, she remained determined to write.

Brewster came of age as a poet in the 'little magazines' of the 1940s and '50s, during a second wave of modernist practitioners. In part a response to a changed postwar world, when women were increasingly present on the literary stage, modernism countermanded tradition, as per Eliot's call for the 'objective correlative' form of expression. Some, like Dorothy Livesay (b. 1909), who was situated at the Canadian modernist forefront, believed poetry should engage the social and political. Livesay, P.K. Page, Kay Smith, Miriam Waddington and Anne Wilkinson all became friends of Brewster's, yet each worked somewhat differently toward expressing self and identity. Of Brewster's poems Robert Gibbs wrote in his introduction to *The Fiddlehead 50* (1995), 'I tasted the bitter and biting pessimism of modernity for the first time', an indication that her early voice had already found its own particular register.

Brewster states 'I come from a country / of slow and diffident words / of broken rhythms / of unsaid feelings' ('Gold Man', *Sunrise North*, p. 75). Direct treatment, unadorned speech, and freedom from restrictive form suited her intent to be of a new 'country'. Her dissertation on Georgian-era poet George Crabbe, who wrote in a frank way of rural poverty, suggests she not only admired his work, but also felt a kinship. She eschewed linguistic fireworks, aiming instead for a deliberate economy of 'language which is clear, straightforward, and with little adornment [...] Nothing requires greater effort, or is more beautiful, than simplicity' ('Chronology of Summer', *The Humanities Association Bulletin*, XXI:1, Winter 1970, p.38–39). As Tony Trembley puts it in *The Fiddlehead Moment* (McGill University Press, 2019), she was 'the first, and thus a precursor to [New Brunswick poets Fred] Cogswell and [Alden] Nowlan, to perfect a style of lamentation that evoked empathy without resorting to sentimentality. [...] Had she emerged at a time more accepting of women in the academy she would have taken a place at UNB next to the *Fiddlehead* male principals.' But that time hadn't yet arrived; she was on her own.

In her collection *Spring Again*, a finalist for the 1991 Pat Lowther Award and dedicated to Livesay, Page, Smith and Waddington, Brewster's poem 'Nobody' begins: 'Odysseus and Ezra Pound might be Noman: / What about Dorothy Pound, Olga Rudge, / Penelope, Circe, Nausicaa, Helen? [...] Did any of these women think themselves nobodies? / What sort of a poem would Helen of Troy have written...?' (p. 17) Taking cues from Virginia Woolf and Katherine Mansfield, Brewster recreated and reconnected with that Other. By melding the private and the collective in poems that appear to record ordinary events, sometimes with images reminiscent of Hilda Doolittle's, she not only expands the written human experience by representing the silent 'Nobody', but also constructs through the intimate and personal a selfhood. 'In the Library' captures the moment the individual, surrounded by the freight of a culture's history, recognizes its strictures and representational limits. The speaker confronts the contradictions, acknowledging identity's construct ('you are not I'), and endeavours to claim their place ('I am' and 'I am not') as 'the elastic moment stretches' and transforms. This poem, among others, rings with Brewster's intelligence and 'choric echoes' (p. 27) that situate her more precisely in the broader poetic context. In this case, I myself hear something of Elizabeth Bishop (1911–1979), who spent her formative years with her maternal grandparents in Great Village, Nova Scotia. Brewster and Bishop shared a time and place, a love of the Maritime landscape, a quest for identity and belonging, a sense of isolation, and the longing to 'understand / and to be understood' ('November Sunday', p. 17).

Brewster's subjects and preoccupations are often suggested by her books' section headings: 'Where I Come From', 'Past as Present', 'Portraits', 'In Search of Eros', 'Dream Landscape' and 'Devotions'. She gives voice to the challenges of selfhood as daughter, sister, lover, writer, teacher, traveller, and fills the historic silence. She examines death, desire, inheritance, legacy, alongside questions of politics, religion, philosophy, literature and the evolving roles of gender and the individual. Over the years Brewster was also able to revisit and reexamine perspectives. Her later work, for example, records coming to terms with a spiritual change of heart—in her eightieth year she set aside her Protestant faith to embrace Judaism, and her poems become less epiphanic and restrained in style, more questioning and conversational in tone.

This selection represents only a small cross-section of Brewster's substantial body of work (twenty-two poetry collections, five books of fiction, two memoirs, and many other credits over seven decades), illustrating aesthetic touchstones, stylistic shifts and thematic range. While organized by year and the first collection in which each poem appeared, some pieces were originally published elsewhere much earlier. Two particular landmark poems that date from the 1950s, but didn't appear in book form until 1977, are noted in the table of contents, to better clarify progression of the work.

Despite accolades, Elizabeth Brewster has remained at a distance. Whether due to circumstance, her wariness of affiliation, or the persistently gendered view of canon-minders, she has been the poet whose work is included in critical anthologies while her name is missing from their introductions. Northrop Frye favourably reviewed her first book, *East Coast*, in 'Letters in Canada', then omitted it in *The Bush Garden*. This doesn't erase the fact, however, that hers is an integral part of our literary inheritance, one of few long-standing Canadian voices to find a foothold in the early twentieth century's modernist movement, then grow beyond it, into the new millennium. As a poet Brewster 'wanted to save breath / hold it caught in, / not released / until sometime centuries later / [she] might breathe it out / blow the hair of / someone sitting reading / not expecting a ghost' (p.24). As her readers, we might still attend to that breathing and 'play the game of pass it on.'

—Ingrid Ruthig

EDITOR'S NOTE: Many thanks to my friend the poet Brian Bartlett for his dogged literary sleuthing, Dilshad Macklem for her kind support and assistance, and Oberon Press for permission to reprint these poems.

East Coast — Canada

Lying at night poised between sleep and waking
Here on the continent's edge, I feel the wind shaking
The house and passing on:
Blowing from far across fabulous mountain ranges,
Far over the long sweep of the prairies,
Blowing from England over swelling seas,
Blowing up from the populous south.

The wind travels where we cannot travel,
Touches those we cannot touch;
For few and lonely are the sentinel cities of the North
And rivers and woods lie between.
Far, *few,* and lonely …

Space surrounds us, flows around us, drowns us.
Even when we meet each other, space flows between.
Our eyes glaze with distance.
Vast tracts of Arctic ice enclose our adjectives
Cold space.
Our spirits are sheer columns of ice like frozen fountains
Dashed against by the wind.

Drown it out. Drown out the wind.
Turn on the radio.
Listen to the news.
Listen to boogie-woogie or a baseball game.
Pretend we belong to a civilization, even a dying one.
Pretend. Pretend.

But there are the woods and the rivers and the wind blowing.
There is the sea. Space. The wind blowing.

In the Library

Believe me, I say to the gentleman with the pince-nez,
Framed forever with one hand in his pocket,
With passion, with intensity I say it —
Believe me, oh believe me, you are not I.
Making my chair squeak on the chilly floor,
Catching up my pencil, I say —
But of course I am myself
And all the while time flows, time flows, time flows;
The minutes ripple over the varnished tables.
This is June, I say, not yesterday or tomorrow.
This is I, not Byron or Vanessa. I am not in the moon.
I must differentiate my body from all other bodies,
Realizing the mole on my neck, the scar on my hand.
I must wind my watch, say it is ten o'clock.
But I know I am not convinced, feel uneasily the lie.
Because actually I am Byron, I am Vanessa,
I am the pictured man with the frigid smile,
I am the girl at the next table, raising vague eyes,
Flicking the ash from her cigarette, the thoughts from her mind.
The elastic moment stretches to infinity,
The elastic moment, the elastic point of space.
The blessed sun becomes the blessed moon.

Roads

It was one night when we lived at the farm he came.
We were sitting playing dominoes at the kitchen table,
And the dominoes made roads along the oilcloth:
This road leads to Spain, I said;
That road is a Roman road.
The light from the kerosene lamp
Lay dim and yellow on the cracks in the floor.
They were roads, too, but they went nowhere.

He came in from the snow and darkness outside,
Bringing the cold in with him for a minute,
Till Mother had replaced the old overcoat
That lay in front of the door to keep the draught out.
He was a stocky man, not young or old,
His black hair greying a little;
His mackinaw was mended, not ragged.

He wanted supper, so we took off the dominoes,
And Sister told me to bring a plate from the pantry,
And I stood by and watched it being filled.
He had come, he said, from Annapolis, had walked to
        British Columbia,
And now he was walking home again, because
There was no work anywhere on the way.

I wonder now about that man, and whether
He ever reached home, or stayed home when he got there;
Whether he found what he wanted in Annapolis
Or turned and walked to west or south again.
I see him walking down dark roads in the rain,
Muddy roads, dusty roads, wet lengths of pavement
Blurrily reflecting the pointed edges of stars,
Lonely roads with burned woods on each side,
Wide roads becoming the streets of cities,

All mazily criss-crossing forever,
Turning and winding and doubling again forever,
Leading home and leading away from home,
But mostly leading nowhere.

Home for the Aged

The old men sit, five of them on a bench,
Half sleeping, half awake, dazed by the sun,
In the muted afternoon, between one broadcast ball game and
    the next.
Their thoughts are leaves that drift across a sky perpetually
    autumn.
Their hands are folded: they have done with the Sunday papers.

Decorously shabby, decently combed and clean,
They watch with half-closed eyes the passers-by,
The loitering lovers, the boys on bikes, the cars
Rushing eagerly to some scene of active life.

Their lives are folded up like the papers, and who can know
Whether their years passed sober and discreet,
With the measured, dutiful, regular click of a clock,
Or whether some old violence lingers still
In faded headlines on their dusty brains?
What boyhood do they wander in, what middle age forget?
And do they watch their dwindling stock of time
With hope, or resignation, or despair?

Lemuel Murray: Contemplative

'The way to God in our time
is through the market place.'
Nor do I deny the truth or the partial truth;
But yet I pay tribute to
Lemuel Murray, my father's friend,
Old bachelor in stubbly beard and sweaty shirt,
Who in the days when bombs were falling
Sat in his kitchen with its piles of greasy dishes
And read history at the kitchen table,
Leaning his arms on the oilcloth cover,
Stubbing his cigarettes in saucers,
Spilling ashes on the worn linoleum,
While he watched in his mind the long procession,
Alexander, Caesar, Constantine, Charlemagne,
Listened to the voices of Demosthenes or Burke.
He did not wish to use history,
To teach it, to persuade with it, to moralize on it,
To win academic honours with it
Or to get his living by it,
But only to watch the procession, the long procession
Leading to Belsen and Hiroshima.

Afternoon Snow

Snow falls
From the white-grey sky
Soft and weary;
Snow falls, and my heart is sad.
I have closed my room from the weather;
I have bought chrysanthemums,
Small yellow suns in the winter room;
But snow falls, and the world is wrapped in grey.
The afternoon lengthens and grows dim.
My eyes are giddy from watching the window.
I want you to come, and am afraid you may.
You might walk past, in the soft dark street,
And I would never know.

November Sunday

I awoke tired
having dreamed of you,
but I cannot remember the dream.

Beyond my window
beyond the city
there are fields
and the fields roll eastward.
I see in my mind
cars driving
the wide flat highways
towards home.

I wonder again, as always,
if I truly love you
or if only my breasts love you,
wanting your hand.

Can I analyse longing
or weigh desire,
dispel an illusion
by reducing it to so much chemistry,
an attraction of atoms for atoms?

I admit I do not understand you.

Nor do you understand me.
My mind has caves
secret and deep
and darkly shaded.
If you came in
you might be lost there
forever.
I also might be lost
exploring you,

might forget the boundaries
of my own selfhood.

To understand
and to be understood
and yet to be beloved
in spite of understanding
or because of it
is, I suppose,
what we all want.

Yet another person
is an island world
alien, dangerous.
All around the shores
are piercing rocks
and on the branches of the flowering trees
are thorns that thirst for blood.

Blueflag

So that I would not pick the blueflag
in the midst of the pond
(and get my clothes wet)
my mother told me that it was poison.

I watched this beautiful, frightening flower
growing up from the water
from its green reeds,
washed blue, sunveined,
and wanted it more
than all the flowers I was allowed to pick,
wild roses, pink and smooth as soap,
or the milk-thin daisies
with butterblob centres.

I noticed that the midges
that covered the surface of the water
were not poisoned by the blueflag,
but I thought they must have
a different kind of life from mine.

Even now, if I pick one,
fear comes over me, a trembling.
I half expect to be struck dead
by the flower's magic

a potency seeping
from its dangerous blue skin
its veined centre.

Inheritance

As a child I overheard my deaf father
talking to himself, wondering
where the next meal was coming from, saying
'All's lost,' saying
'What will we do?'
Saying, 'They'd be better off without me.'

And I followed him about dumbly,
wishing to say 'I love you'
fearing where he might walk
or what he might do
wishing to make him successful
brilliant and admired,

and not this shabby man
with mended trousers
and scuffed shoes
stumbling apologetically about the house.

2

He was a good man, my father,
a childlike man,
never given to violence, afraid of blood,
afraid of hurting others, a gentle man;
yet I think I was ashamed of him a little
because he never won in life,
also because he tried to comfort himself
by pretending to despise those who prospered,
and because he talked too loudly
and repeated the same jokes many times.

But I could never cut him out of myself,
my argumentative, mild father,
arrogant and timid.

Sometimes lately
I find I also repeat the same jokes.

3

My mother was always hunting for four-leaf clovers,
and, since her eyes were quick, she found many.
They were stuffed in all her books and Bibles,
but she complained to me once
that they did not bring her luck.

I repeated her words to a neighbour
and she rebuked me later.

'Never tell anyone outside the family'
she warned me then,
'that any of us don't think we are lucky.'

4

Green was my mother's favourite colour,
colour of grass and hope.
All her life she wanted
a green velvet dress
and never had one.

Bridge

I remember walking the bridge across the river
one evening in spring with my mother
when I was thirteen.
We took turns carrying a suitcase
which had in it just about all we owned,
and we were not sure with which relatives
we might spend the night.
It was a high, clear evening,
with the new moon out and all the stars,
and we stopped halfway over the bridge
to look down into the quiet water
so still and so deep.

I thought my mother,
who liked beautiful things,
was only admiring the stars
reflected;
but now I know
she must have been thinking
how peaceful it would be
down there
far below the bridge.

Shock

The world skidded, but I stood stock still,
frozen to marble on the marble stair,
while all about me in layers of cold stone
fell the stiff folds of the sculptured air.

I split from myself like a husk, was blown as light
as a queen from a pack of cards, on cardboard feet,
till, reaching the window, I suddenly saw myself
diminishing down the length of the bleak street.

Night Air

'Come in, come in out of the night air,' my aunt called.
'You shouldn't be outdoors in the night air.'
And she summoned us in
from the sweet, dangerous, witching breath
of the evening-fragrant flowers.

Sweet, hot, and damp the air was.
We had played hopscotch in the liquid dusk.
I had just learned three new words:
twilight, honeysuckle, whippoorwill.
Now that night had come
there was no telling when it would be over.

The Poet in the Last Days

I grow too old for love—
have never cared for money—
and fame is youth's delusion,
who read Catullus
and wanted to save, like him,
some one thing—a sparrow, maybe—
from the cold touch of time

a small brown quivering bird
frightened
or a day, night, pair of hands
with veins running blue and prominent,
or a mole on the neck, moved in and out with breath.

I wanted to save breath
hold it caught in,
not released
until sometime centuries later
I might breathe it out
blow the hair of
someone sitting reading
not expecting a ghost.

But I thought then
there would always be books,
there would be
lamps or candlelight,
there would always be people
reading at night,
lonely, stirring up the fire,
inviting the spirits of the dead

to tell them about sparrows
or the veins in hands
or the feel of a ballpoint pen
grasped in dead fingers.

But how can there be poems
if there are no sparrows
and no people?
How can a ghost haunt
a world without houses?

Where I Come From

People are made of places. They carry with them
hints of jungles or mountains, a tropic grace
or the cool eyes of sea-gazers. Atmosphere of cities
how different drops from them, like the smell of smog
or the almost-not-smell of tulips in the spring,
nature tidily plotted in little squares
with a fountain in the centre; museum smell,
art also tidily plotted with a guidebook;
or the smell of work, glue factories maybe,
chromium-plated offices; smell of subways
crowded at rush hours.

              Where I come from, people
carry woods in their minds, acres of pine woods;
blueberry patches in the burned-out bush;
wooden farmhouses, old, in need of paint,
with yards where hens and chickens circle about,
clucking aimlessly; battered schoolhouses
behind which violets grow. Spring and winter
are the mind's chief seasons: ice and the breaking of ice.

A door in the mind blows open, and there blows
a frosty wind from fields of snow.

Woman on a Bus: In New Brunswick Woods

No, I'm not used to it yet, though it's over forty years.
My husband was a soldier in the War,
came from these parts. You know how it was in the War.
We were sorry for the boys so far from home,
and England was dreary then, with all the rationing,
and the cold, and the shortages. This country sounded good,
and Ed looked good in uniform. He said I'd never be sorry.

Look at all those woods. Ed thought it pretty country,
but I never got used to all that fir and spruce
and the trees going on for miles and miles.
Not the kind of woods you walk in, like at home.

I used to walk in the woods when I first came over,
go out and sing to myself there, but they thought I was crazy,
and so I stopped. My, how I used to cry
back in those early days. Some women went back;
but there — I'd married Ed, and I'd stick by him.

Well, he was a good man in his way,
never got drunk to speak of, never swore
when I was around. He couldn't help the country
being the way it is.

                What I really wanted
was something, now, like Brighton.
I had a holiday there when I was young —
stayed nearly a week — that was a jolly time.
Brighton was grand. That's when I was in service
not far from there. But there's nothing like that here.

Look at the dark, how it's come on so sudden.
They have no twilight here, as they have at home.
She dips and is gone. There are no softnesses,
but only black and brightness.

No, even the violets here don't have the smell
they did at home, when you walked down the road
in the April night and smelled them.

Now that Ed's gone, I think sometimes of going
back home and seeing it. But I'm afraid
maybe the country isn't what it was.
I wouldn't know my sisters. All my children
live in these parts. And maybe —
I don't know —
when I got over there I'd miss the woods.

On Reading Another Poet

I think we are being given the same messages
that oracles are speaking in our dreams
warning admonition code
syllables of unknown meaning.

We are not in competition.
If I say the same thing
it is not because I copy
but because the voice says so.

Maybe there will be hundreds of us
like choric echoes.
It will not matter
that the words repeat themselves

so long as what is said
rises like the tide in all our separate waves
and beats upon and shapes the dreaming shore.

Tired of Books

Tired of books

I don't want to write
literature
the stuff students are examined on

just notes

a few memories

as my father told me his:
that teacher who threw a slate at him
which just missed his head
and stuck in the wall

a few dreams and trances

my mother sleepwalking
down the road in a white flannel nightgown
with my uncles walking after her
to see that she came to no harm

scraps scraps
no wisdom.

Whatever you do
it'll all be the same a hundred years from now
my father said

could be right

or maybe it's the other way around:
whatever you do
lasts forever

the slate thrown at my father
still firmly wedged
in my bleeding forehead
just behind my eyes

When I Am Old

When I am old
I think
I shall move to Victoria

with all these others.
I'll find a few rooms to live in
somewhere overlooking
one of the bays,
with a twisted oak
growing in the yard.

My own limbs too will be gnarled and twisted.
I shall let my hair go grey,
and I'll eat as many meringues as I want
from the Dutch sweet shop
at the corner of Fort and Douglas
and not worry at all about growing fat.
I shall walk with a cane
heavily

on the sidewalk
or along the paths of the park
carrying a brown paper-bag full of breadcrumbs
to feed the swans on the lake
or the gulls or pigeons.

On my kitchen table
I'll keep a brown pot filled with narcissi,
and on the walls of my bedroom
where I can see it first thing in the morning
a picture of snowy prairies
under a blue sky.

I'll go to Quaker meetings
and potluck suppers

and the Spirit will speak through me
quoting Bible texts
scraps of Plotinus
and my mother's old recipes.

And at long last I shall write
the great poem I have not yet written
the wise summation
of the life I have lived
and have not managed to live

with the voice of two oceans
with the voice of the prairie wind
the caw of crows
and seagulls screaming

And I shall no longer care
if I am loved or famous
or good or clever.
It will be enough to be,
to have been, to speak
to myself
and anyone else
who may overhear

living from one day
to another
as only children live
and the very old

on the shores
of the widest ocean

anywhere

'The World Is My Country'

Outside my hotel window
the pink and yellow light of morning
colours the clouds over
the chimney tops of Sydney.

The squeaking chattering birds
circle with harsh voices
        (I too have just alit
        after a long night's flight
        across water)

traffic hums
and I hear hoarse
human cries.

Now in that gold mass
behind the highrise
it must be the sun coming
over the little white sailboats
in the bay
and all the strip joints of King's Cross.

At home in Canada
I suppose it's still
yesterday
late winter or early spring
while here it's summer
steaming — though they call it autumn.

There: the sun's up now
        revealed
so bright I turn away
blinded and dazzled by
this gold wafer dangling
divine, dangerous

cause of sunburn, headaches, thirst
but source of all
that makes this planet home

            my native land
and me earthling
no alien
wherever sun and water meet

however turned the season

In Wellington, for Katherine Mansfield

A cold, sullen afternoon in Wellington —
late March — late autumn —
Saturday afternoon, with all the shops closed
so tight I can't even buy a postcard

in your home town, K.M.
(born Kathleen Beauchamp
in this city of ugly buildings
and beautiful bays)

I have taken the tourist bus
up all those winding streets
where the houses perch on cliffs
like nests above the water
and down roads past craggy beaches
where the waves dash foaming
against the shore

(On a dull street in the New Town
the driver said,
'This street's called Mansfield
after the famous poet';
and I knew without asking
she had never read your work)

And now, the drive over, nothing to do,
tired of walking
through windy streets in the half-drizzle
past all the shuttered shops and lunchrooms,
I come back to my hotel on Lambton Quay
(where you once stood reading
one of your first stories
in a newspaper)

I snuggle from the chill
under the eiderdown,

propped up with pillows,
reading scraps of your letters

written also in hotel rooms
alone in foreign countries
while you cuddled a hot-water bottle
or a fat
Dickens novel
to drive away the nightmare
or jotted the price of your meals
in the back of your notebook
next to the hints for stories.

Last night there was thunder
and lightning flashing.
There were huge gusts of wind
and the rain came by bucketsful

and there were people screaming in the street
outside my window
as if for help or in anger

And I thought of you torn out of life
pretending happiness and serenity
but really screaming (silently) for help,
angry, fearful, not sure you were beloved,
not satisfied with your stories

('I want much more material'
you said, 'I am tired of my little stories
like birds bred in cages')

wanting life, health, gardens, babies
to replace those lost,
wanting to see New Zealand again,
wanting time, time, a whole lifetime

And while you were dying
gasping in your eagerness for life

I was a child in the cradle
mindless as a plant
floating in air
knowing nothing
caring for nothing
the pale January sun touching
my small fingers clenched
above the white wool coverlet
as I breathed in
breathed out
easily

no trouble at all

Adjusting to Disaster

The surprising thing is how usual
it seems, walking to work
through purple snow; and how unremarkable
the two-headed monsters peering
at night through the kitchen window.
Even the walks through
barbed-wire battlefields
or the hours spent sheltering in dugouts
awaiting the whine of shells
or the final bomb
seem no more frightening
than a trip by bus or tube
through an unfamiliar city.

There is (as a critic might complain
of a rather dull story)
no tension.
There is blood, all right;
there are atrocities
and dragons;
but she, my other Self,
moves calmly wooden
through it all,
like an automaton or a tourist

observing observing
with her filming eyes

For Dorothy Wordsworth

When I think of you, I see
a berry-brown young woman
sitting on a wall
outside your cottage,
mending your stockings or your torn shift
by the last fading daylight of
the sun gone down,
or sewing a child's frock
for little Derwent Coleridge

and I know more from your journal
than from William's poems
about plain living
in the Vale of Grasmere:

the night you could not sleep
for sheer cold
after the peat fire had gone out

the rain coming through the roof
into William's room,
the mattresses filled with rushes,
the kitchen where you ironed,
baked bread, broiled a mutton chop
for William's supper
(you had tapioca yourself,
or maybe an egg)

and there was Coleridge not eating
trying to cure his boils.
William had colds and toothaches;
you suffered some stomach ailment
and spent a day in bed
reading *Tom Jones*.

Outdoors, you pulled peas,
picked gooseberries
which you boiled to eat with tea
reclining in the orchard,
where afterwards you sat
and wrote out fair copies
of William's poems.

You went for walks
to inquire for the post
(a letter from Coleridge
you placed in your bosom:
though it was William, after all,
whose letters you most yearned for
when he was away.)

Delightful sometimes the walks
in the chilly spring
with snow showers in the air

or when flowers were out.
Not just daffodils,
but celandine, violets,
wood sorrel, primroses,
marigolds, blue hyacinth.

Delightful sometimes, evenings
reading together,
William and Coleridge both
full of poetry,
firelight touching their faces,
you drinking a very little
brandy-and-water
and finding yourself in heaven.

Yet, in spite of all those walks
you were plagued with headaches,
melancholia

in spite of the fact
that you were William's eyes
and William's ears
his Muse, his Lucy
his little Emmeline

and though it was you
who talked to the old leech-gatherer
and the gypsy peddler woman
at the door
and the little boy begging for bread

and handed their words to William
for his poems.

The swallows built their nest
by your bedroom window.
One day you spent a whole hour
watching them at work,
their forked fish-like tails,
their white underbellies,
one of them swinging in wind
on the branch of an apple tree.

At night,
after John and William were in bed,
you strolled in the orchard.
The stars came out.
There was a crescent moon.

Coleridge heard
the merry nightingale.
The swallows slept.

One morning you saw
the swallows' nest fallen,
the helpless birds
sitting on the wall,
not knowing what to do.

You must have known then
your world would change;
for brothers marry,
friends quarrel,
poets grow old,
cottages are deserted, gardens overgrown;
the birds nest elsewhere.

You and William read
Paradise Lost together.
You wept at the eleventh book.
('Must I thus leave thee, Paradise? Thus leave
    Thee Native Soil...?)

'O, beautiful place!' you wrote.
'The hour is come....
I must prepare to go.
The swallows, I must leave them,
the well, the garden,
the roses, all.'

Your old age, after all
not, as William wished,
serene and bright,
not Lapland-lovely.

On an Exhibition of Paintings by Mary Pratt

Other people have painted
objects: bread, sunflowers, bowls of fruit,
bottles of red wine,
a red wheelbarrow,
the railway track at Sackville, New Brunswick,
or various views from studio windows.

What's different here
is the female
eye seeing jars
of jelly on windowsills,
a bowl of whipped cream,
ketchup bottles on the supper table,
raw fish ready for cooking
or a wedding dress on a wire hanger
against a closet door

trifles placed
to advantage
in a clear light
all at a point
of repose in which there is still
life.

Nobody (26 May)

Odysseus and Ezra Pound might be Noman:
What about Dorothy Pound, Olga Rudge,
Penelope, Circe, Nausicaa, Helen?

To write the poem is different
from being the object of the poem.
Did any of these women think themselves nobodies?
What sort of a poem would Helen of Troy have written
about the Siege of Troy?

If Penelope had written poems,
would there have been more about weaving in them
than about war and the wine-dark sea?
Would Nausicaa have written love poems
about that handsome older stranger
landed on her shores,
or would she have written about the palace wash-day,
the clothes soaking in the river
or beaten against a rock?
the way she and her maids
splashed each other, making a game of it,
their feet bare, their skirts tucked up
to their knees?

Footnotes to the Book of Job

(four excerpts)

2

Yesterday a friend visited me
who is losing her memory.
'It must be frightening,'
I say to her.
'It's damned inconvenient,' she says.

She too has been reading the book of Job.

'We have to face it,'
another friend has said to me,
'the time will come
when she won't recognize
either of us.'

4

Job is plagued with boils
(elephantiasis, maybe? black leprosy?)
I conjure up all physical ailments:
cancer, perhaps, AIDS, perhaps.
His flesh and bones suffer,
his breath is foul,
he has bad dreams.
He seems near to death,
but cannot die.

'Curse God and die,' his wife says,
but he does not
yet.

9

Can I write about Job on a day
when I see from my December window
the lively boys and girls,
children with sleds,
and a woman wading
through thick new-fallen snow
under a blue sky
carrying her red shopping bag
full (probably) of good things?

10

Postcard from a friend on a cruise ship:
'This is no doubt a palace of decadence:
smoked salmon, kiwi fruit, elegant teas,
live entertainment, and always the beautiful sea.'
But also:
'There are many wrinkled faces,
bent backs, canes,
and one death
    so far.'

Imprecision

My image of the poem
is not so much crystalline —
diamond, snowflake, ice
in underground caves:

it's cherry blossoms falling
on grass that grows and withers,
turns to compost

spring rain rivering
on blurred windows

    though maybe in coming years
    the only beauty left
    will be in gems and icebergs

    no longer clouds in motion
    the shift of seasons
    real apples with worms in them

    the lovely imperfect world
    haphazard
    its wavering
    lines

Circular

How reassuring
the circularity of seasons,
the leaves' gradual greening
for one more year.

The trees throw shadows on pavement
as beautiful as reflections in water.
The shadows sway in the wind.

A woman weeds the flower-plot
in her front yard.

A girl with long red hair
wearing a blue smock
rides past on a bicycle
and returns again.

An airplane flies overhead.
Dogs bark and then are quiet.
There's the sound of wind chimes
on my neighbour's porch.

To the small boy with spectacles
sitting on his front stoop
every minute is special,
watching sunlight and shadow,
the quick flight

of a white bird,
insects of the new season.

The whole world
(he imagines —
I imagine)
is a sundial
telling of time's past
revolutions,
future prospects.

Leaves of yesterday's newspaper
blow on the wind carrying
what singular
familiar narratives?

Song for an Exodus

Word beyond words,
speak to me in the silences.
Light beyond sun and stars,
shine in my darkness.

Be to me dewfall
drenching the desert;
manna at dawning,
eventide's rest.

Be law, be freedom,
be rock, be cloud-drift,
be fire and wind,
the ripple of grass

valley of shadow,
mountain of vision,
journey's beginning,
journey's end.

Dandelion Spring

It's the dandelions
that make me believe it's spring,
not those other blossoms —
of cherries, pears, whatever —
that bloom here early anyway,
even in February.

It's the veil of green
just hovering over the trees

the small, chittering birds
(sparrows, are they?)
hopping about on hedges.

It's the boy with the kite
escaping from him

some feeling in the air
that makes it seem possible
life might go on forever

the spirit leap in air
like a kite
soaring above the trees.

Santiago de Compostela

Whan that Aprille with his shoures soote
The droghte of March hath perced to the roote ...
Thanne longen folk to goon on pilgrimages
        —Chaucer, *Canterbury Tales*, Prologue

The Wife of Bath came here,
as she came to Canterbury, Rome, Jerusalem.
Does that mean Chaucer came here, maybe?

I look across at the Cathedral
from the hotel opposite.
Rain is pouring down,
drenching the crowds of pilgrim-tourists
in spite of their mushrooming umbrellas.
I don't intend to climb those sixty steps
into the Cathedral.
My Puritan ancestors would disapprove
of all that statuary and stained glass,
the fol-de-rols of faith.

If I'm a pilgrim here,
it's not for the bones of St. James,
which I can't truly believe are preserved
so far from where he died.
It's for the Wife of Bath,
a fictive saint of another sort,
who was happy to have had
her world as in her time
(however dangerous that mediaeval world was).

Did she come here in search
of her sixth husband?
Would she have climbed those steps,
or would she have stayed in the hotel,
drinking spiced wine, talking to another pilgrim,
telling or hearing a story?

I sit in the coffee shop,
drink hot chocolate
against the chill of the day,
talk to a couple from Yorkshire
who visited here before
in sunny weather.
'We sat in the square,' the wife says,
'and ate scrambled eggs. They were delicious.'
A woman walks past
grumbling that she can't find
her usual brand of cigarettes.

April or September,
why do we travel?
Restlessness hits,
a yearning for oceans, mountains,
mosques, cathedrals, stave churches,
temples to the thunder god

mysterious old bones:
St. James or the bog man
preserved near Aarhus,
or Chaucer entombed in Westminster.

We're homesick for our past
or cave or pyramid,
our future on other planets,
something unattainable
as a perfect poem or as the Wife of Bath's
final beloved husband.

We want connections
to our once and future footprints
in the shady groves of Eden.

Still, here we sit
on a rainy morning in Spain,
drinking our café au lait, espresso or hot chocolate,
pleased to have bought our postcards and souvenirs
and — yes — like Alison of Bath,
in spite of a destination not exactly reached,
glad — moderately glad —
to have had our world as in our time.

Astrophel 2

'Look in your heart and write?' What's in it now?
Not Astrophel or Stella at my age.
Love and battle are for the young,
those filled with foolishness and courage.
Friendship, maybe. Gratitude for good weather,
for waking up and finding I'm still alive
with tea and toast and honey for breakfast
on a day without too much grief.

Yet fear also — fear of gradual shrinking,
fear of living too long,
of aching knees and painful breathing,
of failing eyes, a tangled brain or tongue,
and finally the heart itself a run-down clock
ticking its last astonished tock.

Moody Weather

Rain on the window pane.
Inherited desolation falls upon me,
the weight of my father's dark moods
pressing down on me.

And it is in vain
that I try to console myself
with words of comfort,
saying 'forsythia,' 'cherry blossom,'
'fine day tomorrow.'

I think of that man —
who was he? —
who said he carried two messages
in his coat pockets.
One said, 'You are only a grain of dust,'
the other, 'The world was made for you.'

Both believable, in their way,
but dark clouds
and the raven's hoarse call
may make the grain of dust in one pocket
outweigh the shiny world in the other.

Fear No More

Fear no more the heat o' the sun
Nor the furious winter's rages
          —Shakespeare, *Cymbeline*

When he wrote those last few plays
(*Pericles, Cymbeline, The Winter's Tale, The Tempest*)
he returned to the gentle endings
of tales told around a winter's fire
in a country town, far from the city.
The rapt children listened
to bedtime stories like these
while the windy storm
raged outside.

He had frolicked through
the springtime comedies,
suffered the lightning stroke
of late summer's tragedies,
its ambition, jealousy, rage, revenge.

Now it was time for stories
of innocence vindicated,
the wicked repentant or dead,
lost children found,
families reunited,
hostile armies at peace,
those who seemed dead
brought to life again.

The children beside the fire
are almost asleep,
their eyelids drooping,
but are relieved
that Marina, Imogen, Perdita, Miranda
are safe from pirates, wicked stepmothers,
wicked uncles, poison, and tempests.

'Fear no more,' the story teller says,
a half smile on his lips,
almost believing his own words.

Fear no more, the storm is past.
It's time for bed.
Morning comes early.

Morning in July

A July morning
hot but not too hot

strawberries for breakfast
garden fresh, sugar sweet,
delphiniums on my table
white and pale blue
leaning out of their pitcher over
my mother's green tray
a hundred years old.

A bird swoops over my balcony—
pigeon or magpie?
too fast for me to tell.

Across the street
other birds chitter.

If I turn on the radio
I'll learn that the world
is falling down

(Afghanistan, Iraq,
North Korea, Gaza)

but here, for this space, for this interlude
a perfect summer day

nothing more disturbing than pigeons' coo

a crow's hoarse call,
other birds calling out
trying to establish
boundaries
secure territories.

Ghosts

The ghosts intrude

most often in dreams
where they are younger
than when you saw them last
in living bodies.
They wear a coat, hat,
necktie or apron
out of the distant past.
They sometimes walk with you
in strange cities or on forest trails.

At other times
they visit in daylight hours
are glimpsed in the face of a stranger
met in an elevator
or in a bookshop
where old books are sold.

Sometimes you hear their voices
at the breakfast table
or in a restaurant
telling their old jokes
speaking in those familiar tones
you loved or (sometimes) hated.

Is it your desire
that brings them from the grave?
or theirs?
Perhaps two desires meeting?

About Elizabeth Brewster

Elizabeth (Betty) Winifred Brewster was born on August 26, 1922, in the logging village of Chipman, New Brunswick, to Frederick John and Ethel May (Day) Brewster. According to her poem 'Birthday', she was the frail fifth and 'last child of ageing parents // born in one grandmother's house / while my other grandmother was dying / an old woman / and my father sat by her bedside [in Saint John] / telling her they would give me her name.' Following the Great War, her father, a once-prosperous merchant, was bankrupt, unemployed and in poor health. Opportunities were scarce and her 'kind and gentle' parents struggled with poverty. Elizabeth's mother 'liked beautiful things' ('Bridge', p.22) and was 'always hunting for four-leaf clovers' ('Inheritance', p. 20). Of her father, Elizabeth wrote 'he was a good man', but she 'was ashamed of him a little / because he never won in life'. As it was for many who were 'working-class born, Depression bred',* her early years were fraught with uncertainty, illness, constant household moves, and an intermittent education. Her mother decided against sending her to school at age six, because of her delicate constitution, and since Elizabeth could already read, Ethel coached her at home on spelling and arithmetic.

When she was eight, the family resettled forty kilometres south, on 'an unprosperous farm on the Washademoak Lake',* and there, Elizabeth began to regularly attend a one-room school. Though it was 'one of the most beautiful places',* the family was 'always on the verge of starvation'* and lasted only four years. They returned to Chipman, a time she referred to as 'the most painful period of [her] growing up',* and spent a year in a dilapidated old house dubbed 'The Pest House' since it had once served as a quarantine during an epidemic. The local school was now a long walk away and with no proper footwear of her own, Elizabeth stopped going altogether. At times Ethel sought refuge from hardship for herself and her youngest daughter, shuffling their suitcase of meagre belongings from one relative's home to another. When Elizabeth was fifteen her

---

* Quoted passages are from Brewster's *The Invention of Truth*, Oberon Press, 1991.

intelligence, appetite for reading and the idea of university impelled her to tell her mother she'd like to return to school—her parents found a new place to live, albeit in the shabby part of town, so she could attend classes again. In 1938 they relocated to Sussex, King's County, and the beginning of the Second World War coincided with her entry to Sussex High School. During this time, a chance meeting with the young poet P.K. Page bolstered Elizabeth's courage. She applied to university, gained a small entrance scholarship, and in order to give her a place to live, her parents found jobs in Fredericton, moving house yet again. Elizabeth entered the University of New Brunswick in September 1942, where she joined the Bliss Carman Society and, along with several other young writers, helped to establish *The Fiddlehead* literary journal.

Elizabeth's young adult life was not untroubled. Her autobiographical writing suggests she suffered the trauma of an early assault and a despondency she compared to her father's, which culminated in her 1951 attempt to drown herself. Given the limited avenues available to her, as a single woman with literary ambitions who needed to earn her living, her life still mirrored that of the child—unsettled and insecure. She took a Masters in English Literature at Radcliffe, Harvard's women's college, in 1947; worked as a teacher, librarian and secretary; moved to Indiana for graduate school; spent a year at King's College, London, on a Beaverbrook overseas scholarship; earned a Bachelor of Library Science from the University of Toronto (1952); and in 1962, gained a PhD from Indiana University. In 1972 the nomadic job-to-job existence came to an end when she accepted a teaching position in the English Department at the University of Saskatchewan, where she remained until her retirement in 1990. Settled at last and with fewer worries, she became prolific as a writer—more than two-thirds of her literary output was published after her move to Saskatchewan.

During the seven decades of her writing career, she joined various literary organizations, including PEN International, held a life membership with the League of Canadian Poets and earned numerous awards and accolades: the Bliss Carman Memorial Award (University of New Brunswick, 1943, 1944); the E.J. Pratt Gold Medal and Prize (University of Toronto, 1953); the President's Medal for Poetry (University of Western Ontario, 1979); a Lifetime of

Excellence in the Arts Award (Saskatchewan Arts Board, 1995); the Saskatchewan Book Award for Poetry in 2003 (for *Jacob's Dream*); and Senior Artists Awards for Poetry (Canada Council). One of her books was shortlisted by the League of Canadian Poets for the Pat Lowther Memorial Award in 1991, and her collection *Footnotes to the Book of Job* was a finalist for the 1996 Governor General's Award for Poetry. She received an honorary doctorate from the University of New Brunswick, a Queen's Diamond Jubilee Medal (2013), the Saskatchewan Order of Merit (2008) and in 2001 she was inducted into the Order of Canada.

Despite deteriorating eyesight and health that began to fail at the turn of the millennium, Elizabeth Brewster continued to be productive. She published another five poetry collections with her long-standing publisher, Oberon Press, over the course of the next decade. On December 26, 2012, at the age of ninety, she died in Saskatoon, Saskatchewan, the city that had been her home for forty years.

Elizabeth Brewster: A Bibliography

POETRY

East Coast (Ryerson Press, 1951)
Lillooet (with art by J.E.H. MacDonald and Thoreau MacDonald, Ryerson Press, 1954)
Roads and Other Poems (Ryerson Press, 1957)
Passage of Summer: Selected Poems (Ryerson Press, 1969)
Sunrise North (Clarke, Irwin & Co., 1972)
In Search of Eros (Clarke, Irwin & Co., 1974)
Sometimes I Think of Moving (Oberon Press, 1977)
The Way Home (Oberon Press, 1982)
Digging In (Oberon Press, 1982)
Selected Poems of Elizabeth Brewster 1944–1977 (Volume 1) and
Selected Poems of Elizabeth Brewster 1977–1984 (Volume 2) (Oberon Press, 1985)
Entertaining Angels (Oberon Press, 1988)
Spring Again (Oberon Press, 1990; 1991 Pat Lowther Award finalist)
Wheel of Change (Oberon Press, 1993)
Footnotes to the Book of Job (Oberon Press, 1995; 1996 Governor General's Award finalist)
Garden of Sculpture (Oberon Press, 1998)
Burning Bush (Oberon Press, 2000)
Jacob's Dream (Oberon Press, 2002; Winner of the 2003 Saskatchewan Book Award)
Collected Poems of Elizabeth Brewster (Volume 1) (Oberon Press, 2003)
Collected Poems of Elizabeth Brewster (Volume 2) (Oberon Press, 2004)
Bright Centre (Oberon Press, 2005)
Time and Seasons (Oberon Press, 2009)

PROSE

The Sisters (novel) (Oberon Press, 1974)
It's Easy to Fall on the Ice (stories) (Oberon Press, 1977)
Junction (novel) (Black Moss Press, 1982)

A House Full of Women (stories) (Oberon Press, 1983)
Visitations (stories) (Oberon Press, 1987)
The Invention of Truth (memoir) (Oberon Press, 1991)
Away from Home (memoir) (Oberon Press, 1995)

OTHER WORKS & ANTHOLOGIES

*Five New Brunswick Poets: Elizabeth Brewster, Fred Cogswell, Robert
    Gibbs, Alden Nowlan, Kay Smith* (ed. Fred Cogswell, University
    of New Brunswick, 1962)
Winter Flowers: for Alto Soloist, Chorus and Orchestra (Nancy Telfer,
    words by Elizabeth Brewster, c. 1980)
*The Ballad of Princess Caraboo: A Narrative of Singular Imposition for
    Mezzo-Soprano and Piano* (Nancy Telfer, words by Elizabeth
    Brewster, F. Harris Music, 1983)
Oxford Book of Canadian Verse (ed. A.J.M. Smith, 1960)
Made in Canada: Poems of the Seventies (eds. Douglas Lochhead and
    Raymond Souster, 1970)
The Speaking Earth: Canadian Poetry (ed. John Metcalf, 1973)
The Penguin Book of Canadian Verse (ed. Ralph Gustafson, 1975)
The New Oxford Book of Canadian Verse in English (ed. Margaret
    Atwood, 1982)
Choice Atlantic: Writers of Newfoundland and the Maritimes (eds.
    Elaine Crocker, Eric Norman and Michael Nowlan, 1990)
Poetic Voices of the Maritimes (eds. Allison Mitcham and Theresia
    Quigley, 1997)
A Matter of Spirit (ed. Susan McCaslin, 1998)
Coastlines: The Poetry of Atlantic Canada (ed. Anne Compton, 2002)
Canadian Poetry 1920 to 1960 (ed. Brian Trehearne, 2010)